Original title:
Our Final Chapter

Copyright © 2024 Swan Charm
All rights reserved.

Author: Kene Elistrand
ISBN HARDBACK: 978-9916-79-227-8
ISBN PAPERBACK: 978-9916-79-228-5
ISBN EBOOK: 978-9916-79-229-2

Walking with Angels in the Dusk

In the twilight's gentle embrace,
I feel their wings, a sacred grace.
Whispers of faith guide my way,
As shadows dance, and angels play.

With every step, their light I seek,
In hushed moments, love they speak.
Each breath a prayer to the skies,
In their presence, my spirit flies.

Through the dusk, where silence reigns,
I shed my doubts, release my chains.
Their luminous paths I strive to trace,
Walking with angels, I find my place.

The Portals of Transcendence

Beyond the veil, where wonders lie,
Portals beckon, spirits fly.
In sacred realms of the unknown,
I seek the truths that light has sown.

Each gate a promise, each arch a dream,
Revealing glories that softly gleam.
With open heart, I take my stand,
In the presence of the divine hand.

Through corridors of time and space,
I wander forth with steadfast grace.
Guided by whispers, soft and warm,
I embrace each truth, each new form.

The Last Echoes of Love

In the stillness of a tender night,
I hear the echoes of love's light.
Each memory a whisper, each sigh a song,
Binding souls where they belong.

Through the ages, love transcends time,
In every heart, it begins to chime.
A gentle promise, a soft caress,
In its embrace, we find our rest.

Though shadows may dim the brightest flame,
Love endures, it holds no shame.
In final moments, when parting's near,
The last echoes will always be clear.

Lanterns of Hope in the Dark

In the depths where shadows creep,
Lanterns of hope, my soul they keep.
Each flicker a beacon, guiding me through,
In the midst of the night, they show what's true.

When despair whispers cold in the air,
These lights remind me that someone cares.
With every step, their glow ignites,
Illuminating paths to eternal sights.

In the dark, no fear shall abide,
With lanterns of hope, I shall abide.
For every trial, a light shall spark,
Leading me home from the depths of dark.

The Gathering of Kindred Spirits

In the sacred circle we unite,
Voices raised in pure delight.
Hands entwined, a silent prayer,
Hearts ignited with love to share.

Beneath the stars, our spirits rise,
Echoes of faith fill the skies.
With every breath, we sing as one,
In this holy realm, we bask in the sun.

Whispers of angels guide our way,
In this moment, we choose to stay.
Bound by grace, we journey forth,
Illuminating the path of worth.

In the warmth of fellowship found,
Each kindness shared, a sacred sound.
Together, we tread this sacred ground,
In love's embrace, our lives abound.

The Divine Prelude to Eternity

In the stillness, the call unfolds,
A promise cherished, a truth retold.
With every heartbeat, the sacred sings,
Whispers of light, the joy it brings.

Moments suspended, time stands still,
Hearts awakened, a shared will.
Through trials faced, faith shall prevail,
A journey sacred, a holy trail.

In shadows deep, hope ignites,
The dawn emerges, dispelling nights.
With open arms, we welcome grace,
In every soul, a sacred place.

As time flows onward, love remains,
Binding the hearts through joys and pains.
In unity, we seek the light,
Together, we rise, boundless and bright.

The Last Scroll of Grace

In the quiet dusk, truth appears,
Written in love, beyond our fears.
Each word a whisper, soft and clear,
A testament held, ever dear.

With ink of stars, the story unfolds,
Of grace and mercy, forever bold.
In the pages worn, wisdom flows,
A guiding light, the spirit knows.

From ancient scripts to hearts today,
The message stands, come what may.
In unity, we find our peace,
In every ending, a sweet release.

Holding the scroll, we bend the knee,
Embracing love, eternally free.
In every heartbeat, we feel the ties,
In grace's embrace, our spirit flies.

Echoes of the Eternal

In the vast expanse, echoes call,
Whispers of heaven, our hearts enthrall.
With every breath, we sense the grace,
A timeless love, a warm embrace.

Through valleys deep and mountains high,
The spirit dances, never shy.
In the silence, wisdom speaks,
A truth divine, in stillness seeks.

Moments linger, eternity spun,
In the heart's chamber, all are one.
Guided by faith, we walk the path,
In love's own name, we'll find the hearth.

The echoes fade, yet never cease,
In every heart, a piece of peace.
Together we rise, through joy and pain,
Eternal echoes in love's refrain.

The Revelation of the Heart

In the stillness of the night,
The heart seeks the sacred light.
Whispers echo in prayerful tones,
Guiding souls to heavenly thrones.

Love's pure essence fills the air,
A gentle balm, a whispered care.
Truth unfolds within the soul,
Each revelation makes us whole.

Hands lifted high in gratitude,
Awakening the ancient mood.
Every heartbeat sings a song,
In unity, we all belong.

Fires of passion, born anew,
In humble hearts, the light breaks through.
The path of faith, a sacred quest,
In love and grace, we find our rest.

With every step, the spirit flies,
Embracing hope beneath the skies.
Galvanized by divine embrace,
In the heart's truth, we find our place.

An Epilogue of Light

As twilight weaves its golden thread,
A tapestry of hopes now spread.
In shadows deep, the light shall gleam,
Guiding all who dare to dream.

The heart's quiet whispers rise,
To meet the stars in sacred skies.
In every soul, the flame ignites,
A beacon shining through the nights.

Every tear yields a lesson learned,
From cinders of regret, hearts burned.
Yet in the ashes, faith is found,
A resurrection, holy ground.

In the morning's soft embrace,
We see reflected love and grace.
The journey leads us hand in hand,
Across the shore of promised land.

In this epilogue, we find our way,
With light to guide us through the fray.
In love's embrace, we shall abide,
With every heartbeat, hope is tied.

The Quiet Ascendancy

In silence deep, the spirit grows,
A gentle touch, the heart bestows.
The soul illuminates each thought,
In stillness, peace is deeply sought.

With every breath, a prayer is cast,
In moments rich, the present lasts.
The humble heart begins to rise,
Toward purity beyond the cries.

In unity where shadows fade,
We find the truths we once betrayed.
With trials faced, the spirit soars,
Embracing love that ever pours.

In whispered tones, the angels sing,
A quiet strength our faith can bring.
As burdens lift, the soul expands,
Bound by grace in holy lands.

In this ascendancy so bright,
We walk together in the light.
With every step, a promise made,
In depth of heart, our fears allayed.

When All is Said and Done

When trials fade and shadows part,
The essence left is love's pure art.
In echoes soft, the truth remains,
A legacy through joys and pains.

Through valleys deep, our spirits tread,
In search of what the heart has said.
With every turn, wisdom unfolds,
In stories woven, life beholds.

When all is whispered, and vows are sealed,
In sacred truths, the heart is healed.
With open palms, we let love flow,
In knowing hearts, it starts to grow.

Together bound in love's embrace,
We dance through time, in sacred space.
With grace, the journey takes its form,
In every storm, we find the warm.

And when the final note is sung,
In harmony, our hearts are strung.
With love as witness, we will stay,
In memories cherished, come what may.

In the Presence of the Infinite

In silence, where the spirit weeps,
The heart knows truth in stillness deep.
A light descends, pure and bright,
Guiding souls through endless night.

With every breath, we seek the grace,
In sacred spaces, we find our place.
The whispers of love, soft and clear,
Invite us close, to draw us near.

We rise on wings of faith so bold,
In timeless realms, our hearts unfold.
Embracing all, both near and far,
We find the light, our guiding star.

In every joy, in every tear,
The Infinite's love is ever near.
Beyond the veil, our spirits soar,
In the presence of the evermore.

The Apocalyptic Epiphany

In shadows cast, the dawn does break,
Revealing truths that make hearts quake.
The world transforms, the heavens cry,
A call to souls, no more to lie.

As visions dance in fiery light,
We gather strength to face the night.
The past lays bare, our sins unveiled,
In love's embrace, all fear curtailed.

The trumpet sounds, a wake-up call,
To rise from depths, to stand up tall.
The chains of doubt begin to fall,
In unity, we heed the call.

Awakened hearts, we march as one,
Towards the dawn, where hope's begun.
With every step, we shed our chains,
In divine light, love reigns.

The Veil Between Worlds

A shimmering veil, so thin, so bright,
It parts the day from the quiet night.
In dreamlike states, we dare to peek,
At realms where hearts and spirits speak.

The echoes of love, in whispers profound,
Call to the lost, where peace is found.
Each breath a prayer, each thought a spark,
Illuminates the profound dark.

From life's great dance to the stillness beyond,
We learn to cherish the sacred bond.
In sacred silence, the truth is shown,
In every heartbeat, we're never alone.

To bridge the gap, we seek to know,
The light within, where love will grow.
In faith, we trust the unseen way,
As heaven's whispers guide our stay.

A Soul's Return to the Divine

In quiet moments, we feel the pull,
A longing deep, a heart still full.
The journey long, through trials faced,
A path of love, forever graced.

We shed the weight of worldly ties,
Embracing light, as spirit flies.
Through every tear, redemption flows,
To heights of joy, the spirit grows.

A dance of souls, in harmony pure,
Together united, forever sure.
In timeless grace, we find our way,
To realms of peace where hearts shall stay.

With open arms, the Divine awaits,
To welcome back those through heaven's gates.
In love's embrace, we recognize,
The endless bond that never dies.

Chronicles of the Sacred Journey

In valleys deep, the spirit roams,
With whispered prayers, it seeks its homes.
Each step a bond, each breath a vow,
To find the light that leads us now.

Through shadows cast by doubt's cruel hand,
In faith we walk, a chosen band.
The stars above, they guide our way,
In the quiet night, we kneel and pray.

The mountains rise, their peaks so high,
With lifted hearts, we touch the sky.
In every struggle, a lesson learned,
In each return, our souls have turned.

The rivers flow, their waters pure,
In sacred depths, our hearts endure.
With every drop, a blessing flows,
In unity, the love life knows.

Together we share the sacred fire,
Awakening hope, igniting desire.
In journey's end, we shall rejoice,
With grateful hearts, we lift our voice.

A Beneath the Surface Covenant

Below the calm, the currents twist,
A covenant made, a pact we've kissed.
In silence deep, our secrets lie,
Forged in the depths where shadows sigh.

In hidden realms, the truth awaits,
Whispers circle, woven fates.
With open hands, we learn to trust,
In unity's strength, we rise from dust.

The depths may seem a daunting place,
Yet love invites, gives us grace.
Through trials faced, we find our way,
To sacred bonds that never fray.

A light shines bright in waters deep,
In hushed embrace, the secrets keep.
With each heartbeat, our spirits blend,
In every moment, we transcend.

This covenant held beneath the waves,
Takes root in hearts that love enslaves.
Together strong, we voyage far,
United bright as a morning star.

The Fading of Time's Embrace

As twilight falls, the colors blend,
In silence spoken, lives to mend.
Time weaves tales of joy and strife,
In fleeting moments, the dance of life.

Each hour ticks, a heartbeat's song,
Though fleeting, whispers ever strong.
In fading light, we find the clues,
Of sacred truths that life imbues.

Memories flicker, a golden glow,
In loving arms, the past we sow.
Through laughter shared, and tears that flow,
In moments lost, our spirits grow.

The clock may fade, but hearts will soar,
In every ending, we find once more.
For time may wane, yet love remains,
In echoes soft, the truth sustains.

Hold fast the now, let it be blessed,
In every heartbeat, we find rest.
Embrace the fading, cherish the bright,
For in the dark, we see the light.

A Radiant Whisper in the Void

In silence deep, a whisper grows,
A radiant call, the spirit knows.
In empty spaces, love will fill,
The void around us, gentle still.

Each breath we take, a sacred prayer,
In every heartbeat, souls laid bare.
Through darkness thick, a soft embrace,
A guiding star in time and space.

The void may seem a barren ground,
Yet in its heart, the truth is found.
With every soul, a light ignites,
A symphony of countless lights.

We gather strength from lessons learned,
In wisdom's light, our hearts discerned.
Reaching out, we share the flame,
In union's bond, we find our name.

A radiant whisper, soft and clear,
In every shadow, love draws near.
Through endless night, we'll brave the storm,
With hope alive, our spirits warm.

The Last Dance Before Dawn

In shadows deep, where silence sways,
The world awaits the break of day.
With whispered prayers, the heart does sing,
In twilight's grasp, we feel the spring.

The moon bows low, a watchful eye,
As spirits soar, they rise up high.
With every breath, the soul will glide,
In sacred light, we shall abide.

Through hallowed woods, we tread with grace,
In unity, we find our place.
With open arms, the dawn shall greet,
In quietude, our hearts will meet.

As stars begin to fade away,
We dance beneath the shades of gray.
In harmony, we intertwine,
In this last dance, our spirits shine.

With faith as strong as morning's glow,
We journey forth where love will flow.
In every heartbeat, truth be found,
The last dance whispers, peace abound.

Chronicles of the Divine

In ancient texts, the tales unfold,
Of miracles and hearts of gold.
With reverence, we carve the stone,
In every word, His love is shown.

The burning bush, the parted sea,
In every moment, God is free.
With every trial, a lesson learned,
In faith we trust, and hearts are turned.

Through temples vast and mountains high,
We seek the truth beneath the sky.
In every shadow, light does gleam,
In whispers soft, we find our dream.

The echoes of the saints resound,
In every prayer, His grace is found.
With open hearts and lifted hands,
We walk together in His plans.

In every soul, a story lies,
A tapestry beneath the skies.
In chronicles of love divine,
We find our strength, in Him, we shine.

The Last Will of the Soul

Upon the hill where silence reigns,
The soul prepares to break its chains.
With every breath, a vow is made,
In sacred trust, we are not swayed.

The whispers of the past still call,
In memories that haunt us all.
With open eyes, we face the night,
In darkness deep, we seek the light.

As time slips through like grains of sand,
We leave our mark, we take a stand.
With every tear, a story flows,
In gentle winds, the spirit grows.

The final wish, to love and know,
In every heart, His truth will glow.
With grateful hearts, we are bestowed,
In unity, we walk this road.

As dawn's embrace begins to rise,
We part with love, no sad goodbyes.
In every beat, the soul's intent,
In truthfulness, our lives are spent.

Resplendence in the Fade

In twilight's fold, where shadows blend,
We seek the light that will not end.
With every heartbeat, grace appears,
In the soft glow, we shed our fears.

The colors fade, yet hope remains,
In every loss, love's song sustains.
With gentle hands, we weave our fate,
In the resplendence, we celebrate.

Through trials faced and burdens borne,
In deepest night, a new day's dawn.
With faith as armor, hearts unite,
In every prayer, we find the light.

As whispers of the past align,
In every moment, love will shine.
Though time may fade, our spirits soar,
In endless love, we are much more.

The final breath, a sacred hymn,
In unity, we rise again.
In the resplendence of the fade,
Our souls entwined, in peace displayed.

His Mercies at the Twilight

When shadows fall and daylight fades,
We gather close, in sacred shades.
His mercies flow like rivers bright,
A beacon of hope in the night.

In whispers soft, He calms the soul,
With gentle grace, He makes us whole.
In twilight's glow, we seek His face,
Embraced by everlasting grace.

Each tear we shed, He understands,
In every heart, He holds our hands.
His promises like stars align,
A love that transcends space and time.

With open hearts, we lift our song,
In unity, where we belong.
Though trials come, we'll stand as one,
In faith, we trust, our work begun.

So let us dwell beneath His light,
In His embrace, we'll find our fight.
For even in the darkest hours,
His mercies bloom, like fragrant flowers.

The Last Shout of Praise

Before the dawn and dusk shall part,
We raise our voice, an ardent heart.
In every breath, a piece of grace,
The last shout echoes in this place.

With every note, our spirit soars,
A symphony of faith implores.
In trials faced, we stand and sing,
The worship rises, praises ring.

Amid the dark, a flicker bright,
The promise kept, our guiding light.
No chains can hold, no fear can bind,
In Christ, our hope, we fiercely find.

From valleys low to mountains high,
Our voices meld, our hearts comply.
In unity, we gently tread,
With grateful souls, our prayers are fed.

In every joy, in every strife,
The last shout holds the breath of life.
For in His name, we're never lost,
With every shout, we bear the cost.

The Broken Halo's Return

In a world where shadows loom,
Hope flickers dim amid the gloom.
For hearts once pure may lose their way,
Yet grace awaits, the price to pay.

A broken halo, shattered light,
But still we rise, we fight the night.
With tender hands, He mends the sphere,
Adorns our heads with love sincere.

Through storms we walk, with faith anew,
Embraced by Him, we feel the true.
In every crack, His glory beams,
In shattered hearts, He plants His dreams.

From ashes born, we take our stand,
In His great love, we find the hand.
Restored and whole, we lift our gaze,
In thankful hearts, we sing His praise.

For brokenness can bear the light,
In depths of sorrow, shines the bright.
His gentle touch can heal and mend,
The broken halo, our true friend.

Grace Amidst the Ashes

In quiet whispers, grace descends,
Amidst the ashes, Love transcends.
With open arms, He gathers near,
To cleanse our wounds, to calm our fear.

From embers cold, new life shall rise,
A promise woven in the skies.
With every tear, a seed is sown,
In barren lands, His love is shown.

The path is steep, yet we will tread,
For in our hearts, His light is fed.
As beauty blooms from what was lost,
We find our hope, despite the cost.

So let us dance amidst the pain,
For in each loss, we find the gain.
In every trial, His grace can flow,
Amidst the ashes, Love will grow.

With grateful hearts, we forge ahead,
On wings of faith, no longer dread.
For in the dark, He lights the way,
In grace amidst the ash, we stay.

Threads of Destiny Woven in Faith

In the loom of time we stand,
Threads of grace in God's own hand.
Every stitch a sacred bond,
Woven stories, dreams respond.

In shadows cast by doubt and fear,
Faith ignites, it draws us near.
With love's thread, our hearts entwined,
In His purpose, we're designed.

Through trials, the fabric wears thin,
Yet through struggle, we begin.
To see the tapestry of light,
Guiding souls through darkest night.

Each knot a lesson, every tear,
In His design, we find our care.
Strengthened by each other's grace,
In unity, we find our place.

In the end, the weaver's art,
Reveals the truth within the heart.
For destiny is no mere thread,
But a tapestry of love that's spread.

Celestial Reflections on a Luminous Path

Beneath the stars, our spirits soar,
In celestial light, we seek and explore.
The moon whispers secrets of grace,
Illuminating each sacred space.

Heavenly bodies dance in the night,
Casting shadows, revealing the light.
With each step on this journey divine,
We align our hearts with the cosmic design.

Through trials and tests, our faith is refined,
As the universe turns, so are we aligned.
In every question, a prayer ascends,
As the heart's whispering truth never ends.

With every dawn, hope's light breaks through,
Guiding souls in paths anew.
Each reflection a beacon, burning bright,
In the depths of darkness, we find our sight.

Together we walk on this luminous trail,
With love as our guide, we shall not fail.
In celestial chaos, we find our peace,
In the dance of the stars, our fears release.

A Light Shines in the Abyss

In the depths where shadows lie,
A light flickers, bold and spry.
Hope's whisper echoes in the dark,
A divine promise, our hearts embark.

Through trials that seem never-ending,
In the silence, His love is sending.
Guiding us through the darkest night,
With faith as our armor, we rise in flight.

Amidst the storms, where doubts collide,
His presence lingers, always inside.
Every tear a prayer, unspoken yet clear,
In the abyss, we find Him near.

We hold on tight to what we can't see,
For the light shines brightest, in unity.
While the world may crumble, our spirits stay strong,
For within the darkness, we find where we belong.

In the abyss, we learn to see,
The power of love, setting us free.
With every heartbeat, a beacon of grace,
A light sings softly, our eternal embrace.

The Prayer of the Silent Ones

In the quiet, a murmur flows,
A prayerful heart, the stillness knows.
Voices of those who've walked before,
Whispering truths we can't ignore.

With each breath, a sacred sigh,
Their spirits lift, they soar on high.
In silence, we feel their gentle touch,
Carrying hope, embracing much.

Through the echoes of time and space,
Their love surrounds, a warm embrace.
In moments lost, they shine anew,
Guiding us through, holding true.

Though silence reigns, their wisdom speaks,
In solitude, the soul seeks.
A strength found in the gentle hush,
Guided by love, we find our rush.

In the prayer of silent hearts,
We are united, never apart.
For in each stillness, we're intertwined,
In the sacred breath, our hopes aligned.

The Clarity of the Last Dawn

In silence breaks the morning light,
A promise wrapped in gentle sight.
Each ray a whisper, soft and clear,
Awakens faith, dispels all fear.

The shadows fade, the night is gone,
Revealing truth with every dawn.
The heart now beats with hope anew,
In every breath, the light breaks through.

From valleys low to mountains high,
The spirit soars, prepared to fly.
Where once was doubt, now certainty,
For in this dawn, we are set free.

With every moment, grace unfolds,
In stories written, dreams retold.
The clarity in every tear,
A testament to love held dear.

So let us walk, hand in hand,
Across this blessed, sacred land.
In unity, we'll find our way,
Embracing light, come what may.

Shadows of the Unseen

In quiet corners of the heart,
Lie shadows where faith plays its part.
Whispers linger, soft as night,
Guiding steps toward hidden light.

The unseen bonds that tie us all,
In love's embrace, we gently fall.
Though dark may loom and fears arise,
Trust the compass of the wise.

In every struggle, strength is found,
A sacred pulse beneath the ground.
Through trials faced, our spirits grow,
In shadows cast, true light will show.

The unseen paths we're called to tread,
Each footprint whispers, gently led.
With open hearts, we seek the grace,
In every shadow, we find our place.

So as we journey, hand in hand,
Embrace the grace that life has planned.
For in the unseen, love remains,
A sacred bond that still sustains.

The Last Wish on a Star

When twilight drapes the earth in dreams,
I cast my hopes on silver beams.
With every breath, a wish takes flight,
A prayer whispered to the night.

For every star that lights the sky,
Holds secrets of the days gone by.
In moments spent, the heart does yearn,
For all the lessons we must learn.

So let me wish on this one spark,
To find my way out of the dark.
Grant me the courage, pure and true,
To hold the light and walk anew.

The last wish born from love's pure core,
A promise kept, forevermore.
With every twinkle, hope ignites,
A testament to love's delights.

In cosmic dance, our souls entwine,
Beyond the realms of place and time.
For as I wish, I know it's clear,
With every star, your love is near.

An Offering of Yesterday

I offer forth my heart today,
For yesterdays that paved the way.
Each memory a sacred prayer,
A tapestry of love and care.

For joys and sorrows intertwined,
In every moment, truth we find.
With open hands, I let them go,
In gratitude, my spirit flows.

The lessons learned, the tears we shed,
An offering to the life we've led.
In every choice, a seed is sown,
In every heart, love finds its home.

I cherish all that has come to be,
The laughter shared, the pain set free.
In every shadow, light will spark,
A guiding force within the dark.

So as we turn towards the dawn,
With every step, our fears are gone.
An offering of yesterday,
In faith, we rise, and love will stay.

The Last Scroll of Redemption

In shadows deep, the light does shine,
Forgiveness flows like sacred wine.
Each heart awaits the promised day,
When grace will guide us on our way.

The scroll unfolds, a truth divine,
A whisper soft of love's design.
Redemption waits for souls who seek,
In every tear, the joy we speak.

From ashes rise, the weary soul,
In grace renewed, we are made whole.
Embrace the path of holy light,
And walk with faith through dark of night.

The weary find their rest in Him,
In every hope, a promise slim.
The last scroll tells of all we've lost,
Yet shows us still the gain of cost.

With every word, a truth proclaimed,
Our hearts ignited, forever claimed.
The journey calls, let not delay,
For in the dawn, we're led away.

Echoes of the Celestial Book

In heavens high, the pages turn,
With every verse, a soul must yearn.
The echoes call from realms above,
A testament of endless love.

Through trials faced, and shadows cast,
The Celestial Book, our guiding mast.
Each line a star, each word a spark,
To light the road that's paved in dark.

The sacred tales of old unfold,
In whispered tones, their truths retold.
From ancient times, our hearts refrain,
In faith renewed, we rise again.

The melody of grace we find,
In every heart, a truth defined.
Beyond the pain, there lies the peace,
A promise made, our fears release.

Through hills of doubt, through valleys low,
The echoes guide, in faith we grow.
In every breath, the love we seek,
The Celestial Book, our spirits speak.

Whispered Prayers in Twilight

As twilight falls, the world grows still,
Our whispered prayers, a sacred thrill.
In gentle tones, we seek the light,
With faith as strong as darkest night.

The stars above, like hopes unfurled,
Guide weary hearts in a troubled world.
Each breath a prayer, each sigh a plea,
In silence deep, we find the key.

In moments soft, when time stands still,
Our souls alike, with hope we fill.
For in the dusk, there blooms a grace,
That holds us close in warm embrace.

With every tear, the silence breaks,
As whispered prayers through shadows wake.
In twilight's glow, we rise anew,
With every light, our spirits grew.

So let them soar, these prayers we speak,
In whispered tones, we find the peak.
A voice of faith in night's sweet song,
In love we trust, where we belong.

The Epilogue of Grace

As pages turn to close the book,
A final thought, a tender look.
The epilogue, it sings of peace,
In every heart, our fears release.

With stories told of trials faced,
Through storms and sorrow, we've embraced.
In every heartache, love endured,
In faith we stand, our souls secured.

The grace bestowed, a gentle hand,
To guide our steps across the land.
An ending met with hope reborn,
In every dusk, a brighter morn.

We gather strength from all we've learned,
In every page, our hearts have burned.
The epilogue, a hymn of trust,
In grace we walk, in love we thrust.

Forever bound, our spirits soar,
With every line, we seek to explore.
The tale continues, never ends,
In grace, we find our truest friends.

A Covenant of Twilight

In the dusk where shadows play,
Faith is born in gentle sway.
Whispers dance on evening air,
Promises linger in our prayer.

Heaven's glow begins to fade,
Ancient vows in silence made.
Stars awaken, twinkling bright,
Guiding souls through endless night.

In twilight's arms, we find our peace,
Love flows like an endless lease.
Bonded hearts, we walk as one,
Chasing dreams 'neath setting sun.

In stillness, truth is clearly shown,
In every heart, the light has grown.
Through seasons' change, we hold our place,
Bound together by grace's trace.

A covenant that time won't break,
With every dawn, new steps we take.
Through twilight's veil, a path appears,
With faith as light, we face our fears.

Embracing the Divine Embrace

Within the arms of love divine,
We find a peace, a sacred sign.
Every heartbeat calls our name,
In this dance, we're not the same.

Whispers soft, like summer breeze,
Cradled in the heart's unease.
Lifted high by holy grace,
Together, we will find our place.

In shadows cast by earthly fray,
Light shines bright to guide our way.
Each prayer a step, a sacred thread,
Binding souls, where hope is fed.

With open arms, we shall embrace,
The trials that we bravely face.
In every moment, sacred, still,
Love's soft whisper, we fulfill.

Together we rise, our spirits soar,
Embracing life forevermore.
In every bond, we trust, believe,
In divine love, we shall achieve.

The Last Verse of Salvation

In the silence, echoes fade,
A final song, the heart's parade.
With every breath, a truth is known,
The seeds of faith we've gently sown.

Each note a prayer, softly sung,
Stories of old, forever young.
In shadows deep, we find our light,
Forgiveness wrapped in endless night.

In every tear, a chance for grace,
A glimpse of hope in lost embrace.
Through troubled waters, calm we tread,
With love's embrace, the path we shed.

As the sun sets on this day,
We gather 'round, in peace we stay.
With hearts united, we proclaim,
In this last verse, we find His name.

In the stillness, salvation calls,
Through every rise, through every fall.
The last verse speaks of joy reborn,
In faith's embrace, a new dawn sworn.

Journey to the Sacred Horizon

With every step, we greet the dawn,
A journey where our souls are drawn.
Through valleys low and mountains high,
In search of light, we'll reach the sky.

Along the way, the spirits guide,
With hearts of courage, we confide.
In every breath, a prayer we weave,
In unity, we shall believe.

Through trials faced, we stand as one,
With love's flame, our fears undone.
The sacred horizon calls our name,
In this great quest, we find our flame.

With open hearts, we share the way,
In humble service, night and day.
Together, we will journey far,
In faith and love, our guiding star.

As dawn breaks forth and shadows flee,
We walk in grace, forever free.
In every smile, a light bestowed,
In every dream, the love we've sowed.

The Farewell to the Light

In shadows deep, the light retreats,
A whisper fades, as day competes.
With every breath, a solemn vow,
To seek the dawn we cherish now.

Yet stars will guide through darkest sea,
A thread of hope, a tapestry.
In twilight's arms, we find our grace,
Embracing love in this sacred space.

The sun will rise, its warmth will bring,
A promise held in everything.
Through trials past, our spirits soar,
In farewell's grace, we seek the more.

Forgive the tears; let joy remain,
For light shall shine through every pain.
With faith, we'll journey ever bright,
Into the arms of endless light.

Tributes at the Twilight

As shades of night envelop land,
We gather close, a united band.
In gratitude, we lift our voice,
To honor light, we make our choice.

With whispered prayers that fill the air,
Each heart a beacon, free from care.
In twilight's glow, our spirits rise,
A tapestry of sacred ties.

We speak their names, with love not fear,
In every word, their essence near.
Each story shared, a timeless thread,
In twilight's bend, we are not dead.

Our tributes flow like rivers wide,
In memories, forever bide.
The dawn awaits to greet our quest,
In faith and love, we find our rest.

The Last Ink on Prayer's Page

Beneath the weight of final night,
A prayer is penned in fading light.
With trembling hand, and heart laid bare,
I seek the peace in silent prayer.

The ink, it bleeds with hope and tears,
A journey mapped through countless years.
Each stroke a story, every sigh,
In every line, a piece does tie.

For all the souls that came and went,
In whispered truths, our time was spent.
As shadows dance on this old page,
I seek the dawn, release this cage.

Though endings come, our spirits merge,
In prayer, we rise, in love, we surge.
The last ink flows, yet faith shall stay,
In every heart, a sacred ray.

Transcendence at the End

In twilight's hush, we find our peace,
As earthly burdens gently cease.
A final breath, a spirit free,
In love's embrace, we cease to be.

Above the stars, where angels sing,
Our souls take flight on radiant wing.
In silent joy, we rise and soar,
Transcending all we knew before.

With every heartbeat, echoes swell,
Of dreams once shared, of tales to tell.
In realms of grace, we find our home,
Where time and space no longer roam.

The end is but a gentle door,
To life anew, forevermore.
In transcendent light, we join the dance,
Embracing love, our souls' expanse.

The Last Breath of Forgiveness

In shadows deep, we knelt in prayer,
Our hearts adorned with silent care.
Forgiveness whispered through the night,
A fading spark, yet burning bright.

We mourn the sorrows carved in stone,
Yet find the grace not ours alone.
The weight of sins, a heavy chain,
In letting go, we break the pain.

The final breath, a gentle sigh,
Awakens hope beyond the sky.
With every tear, a seed is sown,
In love's embrace, we are not alone.

As dawn approaches, shadows flee,
The soul restored, now truly free.
We rise anew, the heart's refrain,
In every loss, a chance to gain.

With open hands, we lift our plea,
In whispered faith, we find our sea.
The last breath held, we let it go,
Embraced by grace, we start to grow.

Seraphs Sing of Ascension

In fields of light where seraphs soar,
They chant the hymns forevermore.
With wings of fire and hearts of gold,
Their stories of redemption told.

Through sacred realms, their voices rise,
A melody that fills the skies.
Each note a bridge to grace anew,
In every heart, a spark breaks through.

A dance of joy, celestial flight,
In unity, they shine so bright.
They weave in love, a tapestry,
Connecting all in harmony.

From heights unknown, they call our name,
In whispered winds that fan the flame.
With every breath, we join their song,
In sacred bonds, where we belong.

So let their chorus guide our way,
Through night and dawn, come what may.
For in the light, we all ascend,
Together bound, no need to end.

Forgotten Psalms Beneath the Stars

Beneath the tent of endless night,
Old psalms arise, a whispered light.
Each twinkling star, a prayer reborn,
In cosmic paths, our sorrows worn.

Forgotten words lost in the rush,
Awaken now in gentle hush.
The echoes of the ancient wise,
Guide weary souls beneath the skies.

As constellations weave their tale,
We find the hope that will not fail.
Each heartbeat sings a sacred song,
In quiet moments, we belong.

From darkest depths, the light will glean,
The power of what might have been.
Through starlit dreams, the spirits soar,
Their psalms unite forevermore.

So lift your gaze, embrace the night,
For in its heart, we find the light.
The forgotten psalms, they call us near,
In every star, a promise clear.

Embracing the Light Beyond

When shadows fall and doubts invade,
A gentle hand, we are remade.
In whispers soft, the light will sing,
A promise found in everything.

With every step along the way,
We find the truth in light of day.
Our hearts unfold, a sacred thread,
Connected by the love we've spread.

So let us rise, our spirits bright,
Embracing all, both dark and light.
In unity, our souls ignite,
Transforming fears into pure sight.

Through valleys deep and mountains high,
The light we seek will never die.
It guides our path, forever near,
In every laugh, in every tear.

So hold the light, let it reside,
In open hearts, it will abide.
For in the end, when all is done,
We'll shine as one, forever spun.

The Final Offering of Love

In silence deep, the heart does pray,
A whispered hope as night turns gray.
With every breath, a vow bestowed,
To carry light along the road.

For love transforms the darkest night,
A beacon strong, a guiding light.
In every tear, a sacred grace,
In loss, we find the truest place.

Let candles burn for souls now free,
Their echoes dance in memory.
In touching warmth, their spirit lives,
In every joy, the heart forgives.

So lift your voice, let praises rise,
Through sorrow's veil, our love still flies.
For even in the shadows cast,
Eternal love shall ever last.

With gentle hands, we lay to rest,
The final gift, a heart expressed.
In quiet moments, sacred peace,
In love's embrace, we find release.

Ascending Through the Ether

In whispered winds, the spirits soar,
Through veils of time, forevermore.
The heavenly call, a sweet refrain,
In silence borne, they rise again.

With every star that lights the sky,
A prayer is sent, a soft goodbye.
In twilight's glow, they seek their way,
In sacred realms where angels play.

The gentle breeze, a soft caress,
Beckoning souls to find their rest.
In boundless love, they find their flight,
Ascending high to realms of light.

The fleeting moments, echoes clear,
Our bonds remain, forever near.
In softest dreams, they linger still,
To heal our hearts and guide our will.

O land of peace, where sorrows cease,
Embrace the souls, grant them release.
Through ether's grasp, their love shall weave,
A tapestry that we believe.

A Reverie of the Departed

In quiet dawn, the memories stir,
Whispers of those who once were here.
Their laughter lingers on the breeze,
A symphony that seeks to please.

With every step on hallowed ground,
Their spirit dances, joy unbound.
In fading light, we close our eyes,
To feel their love, to hear their sighs.

Through fields of dreams, their shadows play,
In every heart, they find their way.
A tapestry of lives entwined,
In gentle peace, their souls aligned.

So let us pause, reflect, and pray,
For those who've walked this pathaway.
In sacred moments, we shall find,
The ties that bind, the love entwined.

In reverie, their whispers flow,
A tender balm for hearts that know.
With gratitude, we celebrate,
The lives they lived, the love innate.

The Last Lantern's Glow

In twilight's kiss, the lantern glows,
A shimmering light that gently flows.
With each flicker, a story told,
Of love and loss, of hearts consoled.

As shadows creep and stars ignite,
We hold the flame, a sacred light.
For every end is but a start,
In flame's embrace, we find the heart.

So cast away your doubts and fears,
Let love illuminate the years.
In every glow, a promise made,
Through darkest nights, our path is laid.

So gather near, the faithful few,
With hands held tight, we will renew.
In sacred bonds, our spirits rise,
As love's embrace fills endless skies.

The last lantern's glow shall guide our way,
Through every night, through every day.
With hearts ablaze, we now ascend,
In light and love that knows no end.

The Eternal Lament

In shadows deep, the echoes sigh,
A heart once bright, now asks the why.
Each prayer a whisper, drifting wide,
In the silence, souls abide.

The heavens weep, their tears like rain,
For love lost deep, and endless pain.
Yet in despair, a flicker's found,
In every heart, the sacred ground.

Through trials fierce, the spirit bends,
To seek the light where sorrow ends.
Each step a dance, each breath a prayer,
In the tarnished light, divinities stare.

As dusk descends, hope holds its breath,
In whispering winds, we confront death.
The voice of love, a gentle guide,
In every tear, the truth abides.

Beneath the stars, the lost will roam,
Yet in their paths, we're never alone.
For every lament, a chance to rise,
In twilight's glow, the soul's reprise.

A Portrait of Departed Light

Within the frame of memory's glass,
Flickers of joy, like shadows pass.
Captured moments, forever held,
In silent echoes, hearts are swelled.

A canvas bright, yet colors fade,
Life's fleeting brush, a bittersweet trade.
Each stroke a tale of love and pain,
In the artist's tears, the truth remains.

With every dawn, a veil is torn,
Unraveled dreams of the once reborn.
Yet in their flight, a promise lies,
In the golden glow of endless skies.

So gather close, let spirits share,
The tales of joy, the whispers rare.
In every heart, their portraits shine,
In the light we lost, their grace divine.

When twilight falls, the stars ignite,
In every beam, a faded light.
A testament to love's embrace,
In shadows cast, finds sacred space.

Where the Rivers Meet the Sky

In the stillness where waters flow,
Hearts entwined, to love we sow.
Beneath the arch of the endless blue,
Souls converge, as dreams renew.

Whispers of wind, a soft caress,
In nature's arms, we find our rest.
The water's hymn, a soothing balm,
In every wave, the soul's calm.

The bridge of hope, where rivers blend,
A sacred path that will not end.
With each sunrise, our spirits rise,
In the currents, the truth belies.

Across the shores of time and fate,
We gather 'round, no need for hate.
For love flows deep, like rivers wide,
In every tide, the holy guide.

Where rivers meet and skies align,
In our hearts, the light does shine.
Together we'll dance, forever free,
In harmony with eternity.

The Last Embrace of Grace

In fading light, the shadows blend,
With each farewell, new journeys send.
The warmth of love, a lingering grace,
In every tear, a soft embrace.

The whispers of those who came before,
Guide us gently to the shore.
In quiet moments, their spirits guide,
Through the valleys where dreams abide.

With open arms, the night descends,
In its embrace, our journey mends.
A tapestry of hopes we weave,
In every loss, we learn to grieve.

In the silence, we hear the call,
Of all our kin, the lost and small.
Their love remains, a precious lace,
In life's vast quilt, their last embrace.

So let us dance in the twilight shade,
With every heartbeat, love displayed.
For in the end, when shadows part,
We carry forth their sacred heart.

Petals on the Pilgrim's Path

In grace we walk, through fields of light,
With every step, our souls take flight.
The petals fall, a soft embrace,
Leading us onward, in His grace.

Beneath the skies, our prayers arise,
In whispered winds, our spirits fly.
With every heartache, every sigh,
We find our strength as we rely.

Each sunrise brings a brand new chance,
To feel His love, to sing and dance.
In humility, we bow low,
For in our hearts, His light will glow.

Through valleys deep, and mountains high,
We seek His truth, we reach the sky.
In fellowship, we share the load,
Together walk, this sacred road.

The journey long, yet oh so sweet,
In every trial, His love we meet.
We lift our voices, hearts ablaze,
In fervent song, we sing His praise.

The Unfolding of Eternity

With every dawn, His promise shines,
A tapestry of love divine.
In shadows cast by mortal fear,
His light breaks forth, the path is clear.

The stars above, like whispers call,
In quiet moments, through it all.
On wings of faith, we take to flight,
In seeking Him, we find our light.

Beyond the veil, time bends and sways,
Eternity unfolds in ways.
In silent prayer, our hearts align,
With every breath, His love we find.

Each droplet's grace, a sacred part,
A journey traced within the heart.
In every heartbeat, every sigh,
The essence of His love draws nigh.

The mysteries deep, we long to hold,
In faith we trust, in love be bold.
As seasons change, our spirits soar,
With every moment, we seek more.

Seeds of Hope in the Darkness

In shadows thick, where dreams may fade,
We plant our hearts, His love displayed.
Each tiny seed, a prayer we sow,
In darkest nights, His light will grow.

Through winter's chill, our spirits strain,
With steadfast hearts, we bear the pain.
For in the soil of grief we find,
The roots of hope, forever bind.

The rains may fall, the storms may rage,
But in despair, we turn the page.
With faith anew, we rise again,
For in our hearts, His love remains.

In quiet moments, joy takes flight,
As dawn appears, restoring sight.
With every breath, we claim our space,
In every challenge, seek His grace.

From barren ground, the blooms shall spring,
In every heart, a song we'll sing.
Together strong, in faith we stand,
United by love, a sacred band.

The Final Call of the Faithful

As twilight falls on earthly days,
We gather close, in whispered praise.
The final call, a gentle sigh,
To seek the light beyond the sky.

In every heart, a story told,
Of love embraced, and courage bold.
With grateful spirits, hands entwined,
In faith we trust, our souls aligned.

As shadows fade, our visions clear,
With every tear, His presence near.
In celebration, we lift our voice,
For in His love, we all rejoice.

We journey forth, to realms unseen,
With hope aglow, and hearts serene.
The path ahead, though yet unknown,
We walk with grace, our prayers are sown.

In unity, we face the night,
For in His arms, we find our light.
The final call, a sweet embrace,
Together bound, in endless grace.

Beneath the Shadow of Angels

In the hush of twilight's embrace,
Whispers of grace fill the air.
Soft wings brush over our souls,
Guiding us away from despair.

In shadows where spirits abound,
Light breaks through in gentle streams.
Heaven's promise lingers bright,
As we walk through faith-filled dreams.

Sorrow fades in love's warm glow,
Each tear transforms into prayer.
Beneath the shadow, we find peace,
As angels wrap us with care.

Hearts uplifted, worries cease,
In this sacred, holy space.
Together, we stand hand in hand,
Beneath the shadow of grace.

In every struggle, hope remains,
In every storm, God's light shines.
Beneath the shadow of love's call,
Each soul learns to intertwine.

The Last Breath of Faith

When the night begins to fall,
And hope is but a flickering flame,
We gather strength in whispered prayer,
Trusting in our Savior's name.

The winds of doubt may howl and roar,
Yet courage blooms amidst the strife.
In the quiet, a still voice calls,
Reminding us of eternal life.

With every sigh, a promise grows,
In every heart, a lantern glows.
The last breath of faith shall rise,
As clouds part to unveil the skies.

In the shadows of what we fear,
Hope stands tall, unwavering, bright.
The last breath may come to us all,
Yet faith endures beyond the night.

As we face the great unknown,
Love will guide us, true and kind.
The last breath of faith will lead,
To a future we'll surely find.

Redemption in the Silence

In the stillness, spirits rise,
Searching for the sacred sound.
In the silence, hearts are mended,
In the calm, lost souls are found.

Hope emerges in quiet tears,
Each drop a testament of grace.
In the void, redemption stirs,
Healing scars that time can trace.

Beneath the weight of weary days,
Soft whispers beckon from above.
In the silence, we rediscover,
The boundless depths of divine love.

With every breath, we seek the light,
Illuminating paths of peace.
In the silence, faith takes flight,
And all our burdens shall cease.

In shadows deep, we find our way,
For silence speaks in sacred ways.
Redemption blooms in quiet places,
As love transforms our darkest days.

As the Sun Sets on Eternity

As the sun dips low and sighs,
Casting gold upon the sea,
We reflect on our journey,
In search of what will ever be.

Each moment, a thread in time,
Woven with the hands of fate.
In twilight's grace, we pause and think,
Of love's embrace that we await.

The horizon whispers tales untold,
Of souls aligned in sacred trust.
As shadows lengthen, hearts unite,
In hope and faith, we find our just.

As the stars begin to shine above,
Dreams flicker like celestial sparks.
In every dusk, there lies a dawn,
As the light transforms our hearts.

With each setting sun, we learn anew,
That eternity is not far.
In every end, a beginning glows,
As love's light leads us where we are.

The Golden Hour of Grace

In twilight's glow, the shadows bend,
Soft whispers carry, hearts they mend.
At day's last breath, grace fills the air,
In every spirit, love and prayer.

A sacred hour, our souls unite,
With humble hands, we seek the light.
In reverence, we bow and sing,
Echoing the hope that faith can bring.

The sun retreats, a golden hue,
Illuminates what we hold true.
With open hearts, we share our plight,
Embracing peace in the coming night.

In each heartbeat, God's mercy flows,
A promise held where harmony grows.
With gratitude, our spirits soar,
In this hour, we seek no more.

As candles flicker, prayers arise,
In every tear, the soul replies.
In gentle silence, faith bestows,
The golden hour, where grace glows.

Intercession at Dusk

As dusk descends, our voices blend,
In earnest prayer, our hearts we send.
With fervent hope, we plead our case,
To find in Him, abundant grace.

The stars awaken, watchful, bright,
Guiding our thoughts through the silent night.
In quiet whispers, our needs unfold,
Each prayer a story, tenderly told.

We gather close, the world undone,
In unity, our battles won.
With every word, we seek His face,
In this communion, we find our place.

The heavens open, blessings flow,
In every heart, a flame aglow.
Through intercession, burdens lift,
In loving kindness, we find the gift.

When shadows fall, and doubts surround,
In prayerful hearts, our strength is found.
Together we stand, as dusk unfolds,
With faith unwavering, the spirit molds.

The Silence of a Thousand Prayers

In the stillness, a whisper dwells,
A chorus formed of sacred spells.
From every heart, the silence sings,
The depth of hope that fervor brings.

A tapestry of dreams alight,
Woven in thoughts, both day and night.
The quiet strength of souls ablaze,
In silent witness, our spirits raise.

Each unspoken prayer finds its home,
In graced embrace, where we roam.
In tranquil trust, we cast our cares,
And find within, the peace that dares.

The stillness speaks, and hearts align,
In every pause, a sign divine.
A thousand prayers, a sacred flow,
In silence profound, our spirits grow.

In sacred moments, the world retreats,
The soul's quietude, where stillness meets.
In the echo of faith, we hear the call,
The silence of prayer envelops all.

The Remnant of the Righteous

From ashes rise the faithful few,
In trials faced, their spirit true.
With steadfast hearts, they stand their ground,
In every struggle, grace is found.

The remnant strong, they seek the light,
Through darkest valleys, they take flight.
In unity, their voices soar,
Proclaiming hope forevermore.

They carry burdens, heavy and worn,
Yet in their heart, a fire's born.
With every step, the path they chart,
The remnant's love, a work of art.

In sacred times, they gather near,
Each soul a beacon, shining clear.
Through storms of doubt, they hold the flame,
In every tear, a prayer, a name.

Their legacy, a whispered prayer,
A testament to love laid bare.
In every challenge, they find the grace,
The remnant of the righteous, our saving place.

Stars Aligned in Solitude

In the quiet of night, stars shine bright,
Whispers of hope in the stillness take flight.
Heaven's embrace, a gentle caress,
Guiding lost souls to find their rest.

Moonlight dances on the sacred ground,
In shadows of grace, solace is found.
Each twinkle a prayer, each gleam a sign,
A reminder that love is ever divine.

In the vastness of space, hearts intertwine,
Strangers in faith, through the darkness we climb.
With the promise of dawn, we hold each other near,
Under the watchful eyes, casting away fear.

The solitude sings in the still, starry sky,
A symphony sweet, eternity's sigh.
United in silence, we shine ever bright,
One echo of truth in the depth of the night.

Harvesting the Last Fruits of Faith

In the fields where the faithful once sowed,
Golden grains of grace and blessings bestowed.
With weary hands, they gather the yield,
From seeds of belief in a nurturing field.

The sun sets low, casting long shadows,
Each fruit ripens where the heart knows.
In every furrow, a story is told,
Of trials faced and of courage bold.

Together we toil, through labor and strife,
Harvesting hope, the essence of life.
With thankful hearts we gather, unite,
In the shadow of doubt, we find our light.

The last fruits beckon, their sweetness divine,
Nurtured in faith, through the sacred design.
As seasons change, the cycle shall turn,
Embracing the lessons for which we yearn.

From the valley of pain, we rise and we stand,
With each precious moment, hope's gentle hand.
As dusk settles softly on the land we traverse,
The fruits of our labor humble, yet diverse.

The Covenant of Evening Shadows

In the cradle of dusk, shadows gently creep,
A covenant whispered, where the tired souls weep.
With every twilight breath, the promise endures,
Bound by love's grace, our spirit restores.

The evening sky, painted in hues of grace,
In the silence we find the Divine's embrace.
With humble hearts, we walk on this ground,
In the warmth of the grace, where hope can be found.

Each flicker of light shares secrets untold,
The tapestry of faith, in threads of pure gold.
In the stillness of night, our worries grow small,
For in the shadows, we are guided through all.

The covenant sealed with each falling star,
A reminder from heaven, no matter how far.
In laughter and tears, our journey unfolds,
In the evening shadows, a love that holds.

With open arms, we greet the night's sigh,
Knowing in darkness, our spirits can fly.
Each promise a beacon, forever will last,
The shadows of evening, the die has been cast.

From Dust to Divine

From dust we are formed, in the quiet of time,
Each breath a blessing, each heartbeat a rhyme.
In humble beginnings, our journey ignites,
We rise from the ashes, reaching for heights.

The whispers of ages, echoing within,
Remind us that loss can lead us to win.
In trials and tribulations, we find our way home,
From the depths of despair, our spirits will roam.

Through valleys of shadows, we seek the bright dawn,
Emerging from darkness, our burdens are drawn.
With faith as our guide, like the sun we will shine,
Transforming our lives from dust into divine.

Each moment a marvel, each tear, a song,
In the tapestry woven, we all belong.
Our past is the soil for our future to grow,
United in purpose, through grace, let us flow.

With hearts open wide, we cherish the climb,
From dust to the heavens, transcending all time.
In the arms of creation, our souls intertwine,
Forever evolving, from dust to divine.

Hymns of the Departing Light

In twilight's breath, we softly sing,
Praise for the grace the night will bring.
As shadows dance, our voices rise,
To meet the dawn in the endless skies.

Each heart a lantern, bright and clear,
Guiding our souls as the end draws near.
With whispered hopes, we lay our fears,
And journey forth through faith's warm tears.

We clasp the hands of those we love,
United now in the light above.
With every note, we honor the way,
Where love shall lead us, come what may.

The stars are witnesses to our plight,
Their shimmering glow, a sacred light.
In echoes sweet, our hymns will soar,
In harmony forevermore.

When shadows merge with the coming day,
We'll find our peace, come what may.
In every breath, in every sigh,
Our souls entwined, we will not die.

Beneath the Sacred Veil

Beneath the veil of twilight's grace,
We seek the truth in love's embrace.
With open hearts and eyes so clear,
We find the light that draws us near.

The whispers call from realms unknown,
Where fragile spirits gently roam.
In sacred silence, we embrace,
The tender warmth of love's pure face.

Each tear we shed, a testament,
To lives lived full, to moments spent.
In sacred circles, time unbends,
Eternal love that never ends.

With faith like stars that brightly gleam,
We wander paths within our dream.
Enwrapped in hope, we rise above,
United always in endless love.

From earth to sky, our spirits fly,
Beneath the veil, we cannot die.
In whispered prayers, we find our way,
Forever shining, night and day.

A Revelation Unfolding

In shadows deep, the truth reveals,
A mystery spun from love's great wheels.
With every heartbeat, wisdom flows,
In quiet moments, our spirit grows.

A tapestry of dreams we weave,
In every strand, the past we leave.
As veils are lifted, bright and bold,
A revelation, our souls unfold.

In unity, our voices blend,
A sacred song that has no end.
Through trials faced, we stand as one,
Our journey leads us to the sun.

With courage bright, we seek the grace,
Of love eternal, our sacred place.
With every step, we rise and shine,
In faith unbroken, our hearts align.

From darkness born, we claim the light,
In every sorrow, in every fight.
A revelation, pure and true,
In all we are and all we do.

The Last Testament of the Soul

In twilight's calm, we pen our fate,
With hearts aflame, we contemplate.
What truths remain, what love we share,
In every breath, a timeless prayer.

The whispers echo through the night,
A final testament of light.
In every choice, a chance to grow,
In every heart, a seed we sow.

With gentle grace, we walk this road,
Each step we take, we bear our load.
In every challenge, wisdom gained,
In every tear, compassion framed.

As colors blend at day's soft end,
We find the strength in love to mend.
With open arms, we face the dawn,
In unity, we carry on.

So let this testament be heard,
In every action, in every word.
Through trials faced and dreams fulfilled,
The soul endures, our hearts are sealed.

Beneath the Celestial Veil

Beneath the celestial veil so bright,
Faithful hearts seek the guiding light.
With every prayer, we rise above,
Embracing the breath of endless love.

Stars whisper softly in the night,
Heaven's grace, a wondrous sight.
Each teardrop falls, a sacred song,
In unity, we all belong.

The moon, a lantern in dark skies,
With gentle dreams, our spirit flies.
In holy silence, wisdom calls,
Through shadowed paths, our essence thralls.

A dance of souls in sacred space,
Woven together, we find our place.
With open hearts, we seek and yearn,
In the fire of love, we brightly burn.

As dawn awakens the void of night,
Hope emerges, pure and bright.
Together we walk, hand in hand,
Beneath the celestial, blessed land.

The Last Supper of Time

At the table set with thunderous grace,
Gathered souls in the sacred space.
The cup spills stories, old yet new,
In every glance, a love so true.

Time's unfurling like a silken thread,
Binding us close, the living and dead.
With whispered prayers upon our lips,
We raise our hearts in holy scripts.

Each morsel shared, a reverent rite,
The taste of faith ignites the night.
In hushed tones, the echoes resound,
Of promises made, of hope profound.

The flicker of candles reflects our fears,
Fleeting moments, intertwined years.
In every bite, a memory lives,
In the warmth of love, the spirit gives.

As shadows cast where the light once danced,
In twilight's embrace, our souls advanced.
With final words, we find our way,
In the storm of silence, we pray.

Whispers from the Beyond

Through veils of ether, voices drift,
Whispers of love, the sacred gift.
Soft like shadows beneath the stars,
They guide us gently, near and far.

In every rustle of leaves at dusk,
The echo of faith, the promise of trust.
With every heartbeat, the past entwined,
In moments unseen, wisdom defined.

Bridges of dreams, spanning the night,
Connecting our souls to the realms of light.
Through silence, we hear the call of fate,
In stillness, our spirits resonate.

The air thick with longing, an infinite sigh,
Each breath a prayer that ascends to the sky.
In the tapestry woven, we find our thread,
In whispers from beyond, the light is spread.

As dawn draws near, the shadows retreat,
With hope in our hearts, together we meet.
Through love's embrace, we rise anew,
In the dance of the stars, we stay true.

When the Stars Weep

When the stars weep, the heavens sigh,
Tears of the cosmos, falling from high.
Each drop a promise, a wish in flight,
Beneath their glow, we seek the light.

In the stillness of night, the heart's refrain,
Melodies echo, both joy and pain.
With open skies as our sheltering dome,
In the vastness, we find our home.

With every raindrop, a story unfolds,
Of love everlasting, of truths retold.
In celestial gardens, we plant our dreams,
In every shadow, a hope redeems.

As galaxies swirl in the cosmic dance,
We find our place, our sacred chance.
In the weeping stars, a beauty profound,
In the quiet, a love unbound.

Embrace the night, for dawn will arrive,
Through weeping skies, together we thrive.
When the stars weep, let hearts remain,
In love's gentle fold, there lies no pain.

A Testament of the Heart

In silence still, the heart does yearn,
For whispers soft, the fire to burn.
A promise made in shadows deep,
A covenant our souls shall keep.

In grace we walk, though trials be near,
Each step I take, I shed my fear.
With every breath, a prayer I raise,
To honor Him, my voice ablaze.

Through storms that rage, through nights so cold,
The warmth of faith, a treasure of gold.
In unity we rise, unbowed,
In love's embrace, we'll stand proud.

The river flows, pure and bright,
A guiding star, our beacon light.
In every heart, His love ignites,
A testament of divine insights.

So let us praise, in joy unite,
With thankful hearts, through day and night.
In every moment, a hymn we'll sing,
Forever bound, to Him we cling.

The Last Hymn of Hope

When shadows fall, and daylight fades,
A hymn of hope serenely wades.
With every note, a prayer takes flight,
To end the dark, to bring the light.

In quietude, the spirit breathes,
Her gentle voice, a song that weaves.
Through trials faced and burdens borne,
A melody of love is born.

The dawn will rise, oh hearts rejoice,
In every tear, hear love's sweet voice.
With faith as strong as mountains high,
We'll look to Him, our spirits fly.

Together we will stand, hand in hand,
In every storm, united we stand.
Each verse of life, another chance,
To find the strength in love's sweet dance.

So let us sing, in harmony bright,
The last hymn of hope, a guiding light.
In shadows deep, our dreams will soar,
In faith and love, forevermore.

Prayer at the Close of Days

As evening falls, I close my eyes,
I lift my hands to the vast skies.
A prayer unfolds, pure and sincere,
In whispered tones, my heart draws near.

For all I've seen, and all I've known,
In gratitude, I make it known.
For love's embrace, both near and far,
A guiding light, my shining star.

In stillness deep, my spirit wanders,
In sacred space, the heart ponders.
Each moment marked, in love's sweet grace,
Connected all, in time and place.

As darkness reigns, I find my peace,
In faith and trust, my worries cease.
A soft reminder, I'm never alone,
For in His arms, I've found my home.

So let me rest, and find my way,
With every breath, I humbly pray.
At close of day, renew my sight,
In dreams abide, till morning light.

The Final Blessing of Light

As day departs, the shadows play,
We seek His grace at close of day.
With every moment, a chance to see,
The final blessing, our hearts set free.

In gentle beams, His love descends,
A guiding hand, a faithful friend.
Through trials faced and storms we've known,
In every tear, His mercy shown.

With arms held wide, we find our way,
To share the light in bright array.
As twilight wraps, our spirits sing,
In unity, we rise and cling.

A testament of strength and grace,
In every heart, His warm embrace.
With faith ignited, we'll stand tall,
In His great name, we answer the call.

So let us walk, through night and day,
With love abound, we find our way.
In every heart, His light will gleam,
The final blessing, our shared dream.

The Gathering of Saints

In shadows' fold, they come and stand,
With light in hearts, their spirits grand.
A chorus rises, pure and bright,
In unity, they seek the light.

Chanting softly, voices blend,
A tapestry of love, they'll send.
Each life a thread, together sewn,
In heaven's weave, their grace is known.

They walk the path of love and grace,
With open arms, they find their place.
In prayerful hush, they share their plight,
In faith's embrace, they find their might.

With angels near, their watchful gaze,
They shine in joy, their spirits blaze.
And in that realm, of peace and trust,
The gathering grows, in God they must.

All burdens lift, as souls align,
In sacred bond, their hearts entwine.
A heavenly dream, forever true,
The gathering calls, for me and you.

Farewell to the Flesh

In evening's glow, we take our leave,
With whispered prayers, our hearts believe.
The flesh we shed, like autumn's leaf,
In hope we rise, beyond all grief.

The soul ascends, on wings so bright,
In sacred space, embraced by light.
No longer bound by earthly chains,
In freedom's song, our spirit reigns.

We bid goodbye, yet do not part,
In love's warm glow, we hold our hearts.
With every tear, a prayer is sown,
A sacred path, for us alone.

Embrace the dawn, the new awaits,
In heaven's arms, the spirit mates.
Farewell to flesh, we soar anew,
In eternal love, forever true.

And when we gather once again,
In joy, we'll meet, beyond all pain.
In God's embrace, we find our home,
In timeless grace, we cease to roam.

Emblems of Yesterday's Faith

In quiet halls, where echoes dwell,
The stories weave, a sacred spell.
Emblems of faith, both worn and wise,
In whispered prayers, their truth still lies.

From ancient texts, the light shines through,
Each cherished word, a gift anew.
In symbols bright, our hearts align,
With every mark, the soul's design.

Through trials faced, the bond stays strong,
In shared beliefs, we all belong.
Emblems of love, of hope restored,
In gentle peace, our hearts adored.

In candle's glow, the past ignites,
A tapestry of faith's delights.
Each emblem tells of love and grace,
In yesterday's faith, we find our place.

Together we rise, through time and space,
In every heart, the sacred trace.
Emblems of journey, we carry forth,
In every step, we seek the north.

The Final Radiance of Truth

As twilight falls, the stars awake,
In silence deep, the heavens make.
A truth revealed, in sacred night,
The final radiance, pure and bright.

Through trials wrought, the path is clear,
In every heart, the answer near.
With open eyes, we seek to find,
The love that binds, the sacred kind.

In unity, we walk as one,
With grace that shines, till day is done.
The final truth, our hearts embrace,
In every smile, we see His face.

From shadows deep, to light above,
In every pulse, we feel the love.
The final radiance, guiding path,
In every moment, peace shall last.

And when the dawn breaks clear and true,
In joy, we rise, forever new.
The final truth, our souls will sing,
In unity, our voices ring.

A Journey to the Eternal Garden

In the quiet dawn we tread,
With hearts ablaze, where angels led,
The path unfolds in golden light,
Our souls take flight, in pure delight.

Through valleys deep and mountains high,
The sacred whispers never die,
In every leaf a story gleams,
In every flower, a thousand dreams.

We gather strength from ancient trees,
Their roots entwined with sacred keys,
Each step a prayer, each breath a hymn,
In love's embrace, we journey in.

The garden waits beyond the veil,
Where hope ignites and fears grow pale,
With every stride, our spirits rise,
To witness grace beneath the skies.

Together we will find our way,
Through night and day, come what may,
In unity, we seek the source,
As joy and peace become our course.

Pilgrims at the Edge of Time

Upon this road, we walk as one,
A quest for truth beneath the sun,
With faith as blades, through trials we rise,
Onward we march, to sacred skies.

In every shadow, light will gleam,
As we pursue our righteous dream,
A tapestry of souls entwined,
The heart's deep yearnings intertwined.

From ancient stones, the echoes call,
To rise again, lest we should fall,
With humble hearts, we seek the way,
In every night, there comes the day.

The edge of time, where dreams commence,
We stand as one in love's defense,
Each tear and laugh, a sacred line,
We weave the fabric, pure and fine.

At journey's end, in loved embrace,
We find our home in boundless space,
With open arms, the angels greet,
In unity, our souls complete.

The Final Blessing of the Spirit

When twilight falls and silence reigns,
The soul ascends, unbound by chains,
With gentle grace, the Spirit sings,
Of love that flows and sweetly clings.

In shadows cast, we find our way,
Through trials faced, we learn to pray,
With every breath, the truth unfolds,
In whispered winds, the heart beholds.

A final blessing, soft and pure,
In sacred light, we find our cure,
With open hearts, we seek the past,
In love eternal, free at last.

Embrace the warmth of those who've gone,
As night gives way, to break of dawn,
In their sweet laughter, we will find,
The circle close, our spirits bind.

The journey ends, yet does not cease,
For in the heart resides the peace,
With every song, a prayer takes flight,
In sacred love, we meet the light.

Chasing Shadows of the Divine

In every breath, we glimpse the light,
Chasing shadows through the night,
With hearts attuned to whispers near,
We seek the sacred, cast off fear.

From ancient texts and sacred tales,
The spirit guides where truth prevails,
With open minds, we grasp the dream,
In every silence, a holy seam.

Through trials faced, we learn to see,
In brokenness, the path is free,
Each shadow cast reveals a way,
To chase the light that leads our day.

In every tear, a lesson lies,
In every laugh, the spirit flies,
With arms wide open, we embrace,
The chase of shadows, love's true grace.

Together we will brave the storm,
In every heart, a flame keeps warm,
In chasing shadows, we will shine,
With faith and love, forever thine.

Echoing Through the Halls of Eternity

In the stillness, whispers rise,
Stars align with celestial sighs.
Time's embrace cannot confine,
Spirits dance where shadows shine.

Wisdom flows like rivers wide,
With every heart, let love abide.
In the hush, a truth unfolds,
The light of grace, a sight of gold.

From ages past to future calls,
In secret chambers, echoing thralls.
Divine echoes, a sacred sound,
In unity, all souls are bound.

Each prayer carries a holy spark,
Illuminating paths from dark.
Mirrored souls in the cosmic sea,
Connected still, eternally free.

Through the halls, the ages span,
Every breath a part of the plan.
In reverence, we seek and find,
The echo of the eternal mind.

The Twilight Testament

In twilight's glow, we seek the light,
Revealing truth within the night.
Each moment laced with holy grace,
Guides us onward, face to face.

Faith shines bright in cautious hearts,
As dusk descends, the day departs.
In silence, hear the heavens speak,
The tender voice, both strong and meek.

With every breath, the spirit soars,
Through whispered prayers, we open doors.
To realms unseen, where angels tread,
In love's embrace, be gently led.

A testament of dreams and fears,
Each tear a gem, a prayer in years.
From shadows deep, we seek the flame,
Awakening souls, calling their names.

In twilight's sigh, the promise swells,
A story shared, in sacred spells.
Lifted high, our spirits rise,
In unity, we touch the skies.

The Book of the Eternal Now

Within the pages, time stands still,
A sacred rhythm, a promise fulfilled.
Each heartbeat echoes through the air,
In every soul, a story rare.

The present glows with life anew,
In every glance, a sky of blue.
Moments cherished, fleeting yet bright,
In the depths of day and the arms of night.

Here lies wisdom, ageless and true,
In simple acts, and kindness too.
The eternal now, a gift we share,
A mirror of love, beyond compare.

With open hearts, we write our tale,
In unity, we shall not fail.
For every breath is a chapter clear,
In the book of life, we persevere.

Now is the moment, infinite grace,
In every encounter, every embrace.
Together we rise, forever we flow,
In the sacred dance of the eternal now.

Beyond the Veil of Mortal Understanding

Beyond the veil, where shadows dwell,
Lies the mystery we cannot tell.
In whispers soft, the truth resides,
In realms of grace, where love abides.

Each heartbeat echoes, a sacred plea,
To see the world as it was meant to be.
Through darkest nights and brightest days,
The divine whispers, guiding our ways.

With every step, we seek the light,
The hidden path, a wondrous sight.
In faith, our hearts learn to perceive,
The beauty in what we believe.

Mysteries wrapped in the fabric of time,
A symphony sung, a celestial rhyme.
Together we venture, hand in hand,
Towards the truth, eternally planned.

Beyond the veil, in sacred trust,
We find our purpose, rise from dust.
In unity, we dance and sing,
In love's embrace, a holy offering.

Glimpses of Heaven on Earth

In quiet moments, grace descends,
The whispers of the soul, it mends.
Beneath the sky, in dawn's embrace,
We find the light, a sacred space.

Each flower blooms, a prayer unfolds,
In every leaf, His love be told.
The river flows, pure as the heart,
Reflecting beauty, never apart.

The stars above, like angels sing,
In harmony with everything.
A child's laughter, a holy sound,
In joy and love, our hope is found.

The storm may rage, yet peace will reign,
Through trials faced, we find the gain.
In every tear, a lesson clear,
In every smile, His presence near.

With open hearts, we seek the truth,
In simple acts, we find the proof.
Together here, in faith we stand,
In unity, we walk His land.

The Final Call of the Heart

When twilight beckons, whispers grow,
A silent call, the spirit's flow.
Each breath we take, a step toward light,
In every heartbeat, love ignites.

The road is long, yet paths align,
With faith as guide, the stars will shine.
Through shadowed valleys, courage leads,
In darkest hours, the spirit feeds.

The echoes fade, yet truth remains,
A gentle pull that never wanes.
With heavy hearts, we rise anew,
In every parting, love shines through.

The final call, so clear, so bright,
Invites us home, into the light.
Each step we take, though bittersweet,
Is but a journey, love's heartbeat.

Together here, our souls entwined,
In radiant grace, our hearts aligned.
With hope as flame, we shall not part,
For in the end, we're all one heart.

Lights Fading into the Infinite

The sun will set, and shadows grow,
In quiet dusk, the winds will blow.
A tapestry of dreams will weave,
While stars awaken, we believe.

In cosmic dance, the moments blend,
With every breath, we near the end.
Yet in the dark, a spark will shine,
A beacon bright, forever divine.

Embrace the night, the silence grand,
In solitude, we'll understand.
The fading light, a soft goodbye,
Yet in our hearts, love learns to fly.

As worlds will fade into the vast,
The echoes linger, memories cast.
In every star, a story told,
Of lives once lived, of hearts of gold.

In this infinite, we shall unite,
With every soul, a shared delight.
For though we fade, we always rise,
In love's eternal, boundless skies.

A Serenade of Eternal Return

A melody drifts through silent trees,
Echoes of life on a gentle breeze.
In cycles spun, our stories blend,
A serenade that has no end.

From dawn to dusk, the rhythm flows,
In every heart, a seed that grows.
With whispers soft as twilight's grace,
Each note reveals a sacred space.

The laughter shared, the tears once shed,
A tapestry of words unsaid.
In every moment, love's refrain,
In every joy, there lies the pain.

Yet hope remains, a cherished song,
In our return, we all belong.
Through trials faced, we rise and learn,
In life's embrace, we seek our turn.

So let us sing, in harmony,
Of life and love, the sacred tree.
With every heart, we find our way,
In this eternal, bright display.

Echoes of the Cherubic Choir

In sacred halls where angels sing,
Their voices rise, a heavenly ring.
Soft whispers fill the fragrant air,
As blessings flow, beyond compare.

With wings of light, they gently glide,
Throughout the realm where hopes abide.
Each note resounds with vibrant grace,
A tapestry of love's embrace.

The ancient songs of wisdom shared,
In every heart, their truth declared.
Through every trial, through every tear,
The choir's song, forever near.

With every prayer, their echoes swell,
A whisper of the sacred well.
In moments still, they stitch the night,
With threads of joy, weaving delight.

So gather close, O hearts refined,
Let cherubic peace unwind.
For in their song, we find our way,
To brighter dreams and boundless day.

The Exquisite Silence

In quiet woods, where shadows play,
The whispers of the world fade away.
A tranquil heart begins to soar,
In silence, we hear heaven's roar.

Still waters reflect the sacred truth,
In ages old, in timeless youth.
Each moment fills the soul with light,
A gentle touch, a guiding sight.

Beneath the stars, the cosmos hums,
In sacred peace, the spirit comes.
With every breath, we find release,
In silence, all our fears cease.

The world retreats, its noise subdued,
In stillness, we embrace the renewed.
Here, dreams unfold like petals pure,
An exquisite silence, heart's allure.

So come, be still, and know the grace,
Of tranquil thoughts in sacred space.
The exquisite silence draws us near,
To love's embrace, forever clear.

The Final Rite of Passage

Upon the shore, the waves retreat,
Where souls embark, their journey sweet.
The twilight calls, the stars ignite,
Embracing all who seek the light.

With every breath, the spirit grows,
In ebb and flow, our wisdom flows.
The final rite, a wondrous grace,
A tender path, a holy place.

We gather round, hands intertwined,
In love's embrace, our hearts aligned.
With prayers aloft, we stand as one,
To meet the dawn, to greet the sun.

In sacred trust, the veil grows thin,
Where life transcends, and love begins.
The final call, a gentle sigh,
A promise made, we never die.

So let us walk, our spirits free,
In every heart, our legacy.
The final rite, a tale retold,
In hues of love, in threads of gold.

In the Stillness of Reverence

In morning's light, so soft, so bright,
Our hearts awake to sacred sight.
In stillness found, the world is clear,
A moment shared, devoid of fear.

Whispers of grace linger in air,
In reverence deep, we learn to care.
With every breath, the spirit speaks,
In quietude, the heart seeks.

Embraced by nature's gentle hand,
In tranquil fields, we take our stand.
Together forged in bonds of peace,
In stillness, all our worries cease.

The sun descends, the shadows play,
In sacred circles, we find our way.
Our voices rise, a prayerful song,
In stillness, we are where we belong.

As stars appear in velvet night,
We gather close, hearts burning bright.
In the stillness of reverence true,
We find our strength, as love renews.

Milton Keynes UK
Ingram Content Group UK Ltd.
UKHW031320271124
451618UK00007B/185

9 789916 792278